IMAGES
of America

AFRICAN AMERICANS
OF GALVESTON

ON THE COVER: A 1935 photograph depicts the city of Galveston postal employees as they posed on the steps of the 25th Street post office. At this time, African Americans were eligible to work in the postal service only as mail carriers. (Courtesy of George Pete Henley.)

IMAGES
of America

AFRICAN AMERICANS
OF GALVESTON

Tommie D. Boudreaux
and Alice M. Gatson

ARCADIA
PUBLISHING

Published by Arcadia Publishing
Charleston, South Carolina

Library of Congress Control Number: 2013936622

For all general information, please contact Arcadia Publishing:
Telephone 843-853-2070
Fax 843-853-0044
E-mail sales@arcadiapublishing.com
For customer service and orders:
Toll-Free 1-888-313-2665

Visit us on the Internet at www.arcadiapublishing.com

This book is dedicated to all of those who paved the way
before us and upon whose shoulders we stand today.

CONTENTS

ACKNOWLEDGMENTS

We wish to thank the many Galvestonians who contributed to this venture. We are very grateful for their sharing of personal collections of photographic images and stories and for their help in obtaining additional material for this project. Their contributions to this book's photographs will be noted in the credit lines. A thank-you goes to Roland Thomas, who contacted and collected from friends and family possessing personal collections and encouraged them to allow us to include their images and stories. We owe special thanks to Galveston Historical Foundation's (GHF) Preservation Resource Center and GHF staff photographer David Canright; Casey Edward Greene and the staff of Rosenberg Library's Galveston & Texas History Center (Special Collections); Barbara Mallory of the Galveston Independent School District; Ennis Williams of the Old Central Cultural Center Inc.; the Dr. R.H. Stanton family; Sarita Oertling, Moody Medical Library at the University of Texas Medical Branch, Galveston; Sharon Batiste Gillins, Center for 20th Century Texas Studies; Timothy Ronk, Houston Metropolitan Research Center, Houston Public Library; Library of Congress; New York Public Library; Galveston County Museum; and the Texas State Library and Archives; In addition, special thanks to Jami Durham, Galveston Historical Foundation's manager of historic properties research and special programs, for consulting services, and to Dwayne Jones, executive director of Galveston Historical Foundation, who persuaded us to continue this project when we were feeling lost and discouraged.

INTRODUCTION

African Americans are among the oldest residents of Texas. They played a major role, along with Americans of Mexican, European, and indigenous descent, to make Texas what it is today. African Americans worked with other cultural groups to build Texas, but they were still subjected to slavery and other racial prejudices. Despite social and economic injustices, African Americans built viable and progressive communities throughout the state. Immediately after the Civil War, churches, schools, and service organizations were established to provide social needs. Newspapers, grocery stores, funeral homes, and other business establishments that served African Americans were vital parts of these new communities.

The heritage of African American Texans has played a major role in the growth of Galveston. Founded in 1839, the city is located on a barrier island approximately 45 minutes southeast of Houston, two miles offshore in the Gulf of Mexico. People of African descent were some of the earliest residents of the island. In 1528, a Morocco-born Muslim slave was one of four people washed ashore on what is now known as Galveston. He is the first known person of African ancestry to enter the western United States.

During the 19th century, ships from around the world came to Galveston, a major seaport town, to trade goods, auction slaves, and relay information. As the years passed, most Africans entering Galveston were slaves. It has been argued by some that slavery in Galveston was more humane than in other parts of the South, because Galveston was not suitable for growing cash crops. Nevertheless, for Galveston-area merchants and plantation owners, the use of free laborers in cotton fields and in other endeavors meant high profit margins. The Strand, a street in the business district known as "The Wall Street of the Southwest," flourished. Most Galveston slaves were servants, wharf hands, and craftsmen.

Beginning in 1821, when Anglo Americans from other southern states settled in Texas, bringing slaves, the numbers of African Americans living in the state increased. These settlers held slaves as an important source of free labor, particularly after the devastating 1900 storm, when freed African Americans in Galveston played a major role in the rebuilding of the city as well as in the growth of the island in the years that followed.

Galveston has long had a notorious reputation, thanks in part to Jean Laffite, an infamous pirate. Laffite sold slaves in Galveston and along the Gulf Coast in the 1800s. When he was no longer welcome at other ports, he settled in Galveston, bringing with him vices that attracted rowdy visitors to the island. When he was forced to leave, some of the well-established activities remained, namely, gambling and prostitution. This gave Galveston a new label, an "Open City," in addition to being known as the "Playground of the Southwest." Despite social and economic injustices, it has been the opinion of many that Galveston's role as an "Open City" benefited African Americans.

Several of the first churches for African Americans in the state of Texas were located in Galveston. Avenue L Missionary Baptist Church, the first black Baptist church in Texas, was an outgrowth of the Colored Baptist Church, formed by the Anglo First Baptist Church in 1840 for its slave congregation. The property on which the present Reedy Chapel Church (recognized as the first African Methodist Episcopal church in Texas) stands was purchased by the Methodist Episcopal Church South on March 18, 1848, for its congregation's slaves. Saint Augustine of Hippo Episcopal Church is the oldest historically African American parish in the Episcopal Diocese of Texas, founded in 1884 at the urging of seamen from the West Indies. Holy Rosary Catholic Church, the first Catholic parish for blacks in Texas, began offering service at Holy Rosary Elementary School, established in 1886. The church was not organized until 1889. While Galveston is the home of the founding of four African American church denominations in Texas, it has a total of 14 African American churches over 100 years old.

During the Civil War, Pres. Abraham Lincoln issued the Emancipation Proclamation on January 1, 1863, freeing slaves in the United States. However, Texas was the last state to free its slaves, doing so two and a half years after the signing of the proclamation into law. On June 19, 1865, known today as "Juneteenth," Union general Gordon Granger arrived in Galveston and announced to all Texas slaves that they were finally free. Galveston flourished after the end of slavery; freed slaves with limited rights earned wages, purchased land, and began establishing successful businesses. Norris Wright Cuney, a politician, union leader, and activist, holds the distinction of being the most important black leader in not only Galveston but also in Texas and all of the United States during this period. His involvement in the community improved employment and educational opportunities for African Americans in Galveston and all across the state.

Education has been considered by many African Americans to be the gateway to becoming a productive citizen. Even during bondage, learning to read and write were skills necessary for slaves to survive and understand the environment in which they lived. Those who could read and write secretly taught others. In 1869, the Barnes Institute, a freeman's school, became the first school established in Galveston for African Americans. Around 1881, state funds became available specifically for African American education, and two primary schools, Galveston's East District and West District, were quickly established in rented facilities. Central High School, founded in 1885, is Texas's first African American high school and remained the only high school in the state for African Americans for several years. Students commuted to Galveston from surrounding cities to earn a high school diploma; for those who found the commute difficult, parents rented rooms in homes near the school's campus.

While the authors are providing a snapshot of Galveston only from the 1840s to the 1960s, African Americans of Galveston are proud of its talent list, especially Jack Johnson (John Arthur Johnson), who was born, raised, and started his boxing career in Galveston, becoming the first African American heavyweight champion of the world. The African American community also includes among its offspring several professional musicians and vocalists, as well as sports figures, who became national celebrities.

Galveston is known for many "firsts" in Texas, and the African American community has had its share of "firsts" in Galveston. At times overqualified for a position, yet disrespected as well as underpaid, members of the community endured daily challenges. Their success paved the way for those who followed.

One

FROM DARKNESS TO LIGHT, CONTRIBUTING TO COMMUNITY

Jean Lafitte (1776–1823) was a pirate, privateer, and slave trader patrolling the Gulf of Mexico. Around 1780, he and his family settled in New Orleans, where he and his brother operated a profitable business for several years. After being run out of New Orleans in 1817, the Lafitte brothers relocated their business to Galveston, where they continued their very profitable slave-smuggling business. One of their more famous clients was James Bowie, who bought slaves from the Lafitte brothers for $1 per pound. Taking advantage of American laws against the importation of slaves from foreign countries, Bowie would report his purchased slaves as having been found in the possession of smugglers. He would then collect a fee on the "recovered" slaves, re-buying and selling them to other buyers at a profit. (Courtesy of Galveston Historical Foundation's Preservation Resource Center.)

TO THE SLAVE-HOLDERS OF GALVESTON.

In pursuance of a Resolution adopted by the City Council, on the 19th of September, the undersigned, as Mayor of the City, respectfully invites the Slave-holders and those controlling slaves in this city, to hold a meeting

At 8 O'clock P. M. at the Mayor's Office,

ON TUESDAY, 30th Inst.

to take into consideration the existing City Laws in regard to slaves and free negroes, that through a Committee, or otherwise, as to them may seem best, they may report to the Council such amendments and modifications as to them shall seem best calculated to preserve order among the negroes, and subserve the best interests of owners, employers and citizens generally.

The Council is desirous of meeting the public wishes on this important subject; and it is hoped there may be a general attendance and full expression of opinion.

Persons wishing copies of the present Laws can get them on application to the undersigned.

JOHN HENRY BROWN,

GALVESTON, Sept. 26, 1856.   *Mayor.*

Galveston was known as the largest slave market west of New Orleans. Although the market was large, Galveston's proportion of slaves in comparison to the white population was far less than the rest of Texas. Census records from 1860 show a population of 1,178 slaves compared to 6,000 free persons living on the island. The census of 1860 also recorded two free black persons living in the city. In September 1856, rumors of a nationwide slave insurrection reached Texas. The residents of Columbus, Texas, were the first to act, forming a vigilance committee to investigate the rumors at a local level and supposedly discovering a plot to murder the white population of the town. The *Galveston News* reported on the committee's discovery of the planned uprising. As a result, the mayor of Galveston, John Henry Brown, called a meeting of the island's slave holders to discuss a newly adopted resolution concerning the laws that governed slaves and "free negroes" living on Galveston Island. (Courtesy of Dolph Briscoe Center for American History, The University of Texas at Austin.)

At the end of the American Civil War, Union general Gordon Granger was given command of the Department of Texas. A graduate of West Point in 1845, General Granger fought with distinction in both the Mexican-American and Civil Wars. He arrived in Galveston on June 19, 1865, and officially issued General Order No. 3 enforcing Abraham Lincoln's January 1863 Emancipation Proclamation and ordering that all remaining slaves in Texas be immediately freed. (Courtesy of Library of Congress.)

The anniversary of General Order No. 3, known today as Juneteenth, is the oldest nationally celebrated commemoration marking the end of slavery, with its beginning firmly rooted in Galveston. An annual citywide Juneteenth celebration and prayer breakfast is held at the historic 1859 Ashton Villa (left). (Courtesy of Galveston Historical Foundation's Preservation Resource Center.)

At the end of the Civil War, commerce and trade flourished in Galveston, with goods once again flowing into the port from all over the nation and the world. By 1874, Galveston was a banking center; Strand Street (shown here) was known as the "Wall Street of the Southwest." Numerous wholesale houses reopened, along with woolen textile and bagging mills, a rope factory, iron foundries, and factories producing other goods. Many of the warehouses and foundries offered work to African American men. (Courtesy of Galveston Historical Foundation's Preservation Resource Center.)

African American men worked as laborers, as seen in this early photograph of Lawrence V. Elder's roofing company. Located at 212 Tremont Street, the company offered other services, including digging wells and paving streets and sidewalks. (Courtesy of Galveston Historical Foundation's Preservation Resource Center.)

The number of African Americans in Galveston increased after the Civil War, as freedmen moved to the island city in search of work. The wharves provided numerous employment opportunities for African Americans. (Courtesy of Galveston Historical Foundation's Preservation Resource Center.)

This 1880s bird's-eye view of Galveston, overlooking the cotton warehouses, shows the growth of the city as well as the cotton compresses west of Twenty-fifth Street. As Galveston became the leading cotton port on the Gulf Coast, opportunities for employment expanded. (Courtesy of Galveston Historical Foundation's Preservation Resource Center.)

Cotton bales have been loaded on a boat and are being transported across the shallow waters to the awaiting ship in the deepwater harbor, a process called "lightering." African American cotton jammers accompany the bales. Once at the ship, these men would transfer the bales to the waiting ship, packing them tightly into the hold. (Courtesy of Galveston County Museum.)

Available jobs for African American women were mostly limited to the area of domestic work. Women in this industry worked within an employer's household as servants, maids, cooks, and babysitters. Here, a Caucasian baby and a very young African American babysitter sit in the water under the Breaker's Bath House. In general, African Americans were allowed to swim in the Gulf only between Twenty-seventh and Twenty-ninth Streets, unless in the company of their employer. (Courtesy of the Houston Metropolitan Research Center, Houston Public Library.)

In this photograph, the children of Walter and Josephine Gresham pose with their nanny, Julie. The Greshams' home, on the corner of Broadway and Fourteenth Street, is known today as Bishop's Palace. (Courtesy of Galveston Historical Foundation's Preservation Resource Center.)

Sarah Winston, born around 1854, was a slave to a family in Arkansas. She was 10 years old when slavery was abolished. Around 1865, she moved with her family to Texas. She married when she was 19 years old and helped her husband farm land in Montgomery, Texas. After her husband's death in 1932, Sarah moved to Galveston to live with her daughter, Susie Alliniece, at 2728 Avenue M. She died in Galveston on June 27, 1945. (Courtesy of Houston Metropolitan Research Center, Houston Public Library.)

Mintie Marie Miller was born in Alabama in 1852. As a young girl, she was sold to Dr. Massey of Lynchberg, Texas. Her journey by oxcart to Texas took three months. When freedom came at the end of the Civil War, Miller moved to Houston and then to Galveston, where she worked as domestic help for the same family for 24 years. During the 1900 storm, Miller was living with her son, Henry Fields, at 1721 Nineteenth Street. (Courtesy of Houston Metropolitan Research Center, Houston Public Library.)

Amos Sims was born on a Texas plantation in 1851. He moved to Galveston with his parents, Douglas and Mary, at the end of the Civil War. During his lifetime in Galveston, Amos supported himself as a laborer, a porter, and, as he got older, a junk dealer. He died in Galveston in April 1943 and is buried in the Municipal Cemetery on Fifty-ninth Street. (Courtesy of Houston Metropolitan Research Center, Houston Public Library.)

The deadliest storm in American history struck Galveston on September 8, 1900, killing more than 6,000 people and destroying many of the island's buildings. In this photograph, two African American women search the rubble from what remains of their home. (Courtesy of Galveston Historical Foundation's Preservation Resource Center.)

In the wake of the 1900 storm, able-bodied men of all races came together to search for victims and clear the streets of debris, as this team of African American men is doing. (Courtesy of Galveston Historical Foundation's Preservation Resource Center.)

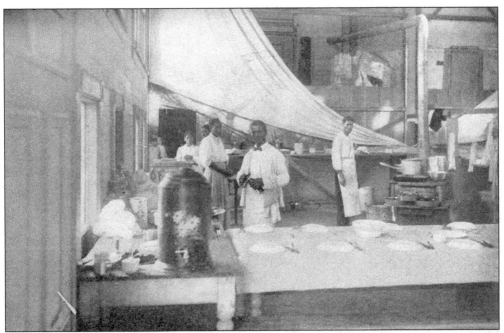

The African American community worked in the days following the disastrous storm, including, as seen here, in temporary kitchens set up to feed the homeless. (Courtesy of Galveston Historical Foundation's Preservation Resource Center.)

African American men in particular were detailed to search for storm victims in the debris. In this photograph, a wagon holds corpses. A young African American worker stands in the right foreground, presumably awaiting further instructions. (Courtesy of Galveston Historical Foundation's Preservation Resource Center.)

Temporary morgues were set up to hold the dead until their bodies could be claimed by family members and buried. However, with so many dead, it quickly became apparent that the only way to prevent pestilence and disease was to burn the bodies. Here, a team of workers, including African Americans, transports a body to the fire. (Courtesy of the Library of Congress.)

African American men also worked at designated commissary centers, set up across the city to help feed the homeless. Food was loaded onto wagons for distribution throughout the community. (Courtesy of Galveston Historical Foundation's Preservation Resource Center.)

After the 1900 storm, a seawall was constructed along the Gulf side to protect the city from tidal overflows and storm surges. Once completed, the grade-raising project began. From 1903 to 1911, sand fill was dredged from the entrance to Galveston Harbor and transported to the residential districts, raising the elevation of the island behind the seawall. African American workers contributed to this effort. Those seen here are manning the end of one of the discharge pipes. (Courtesy of Galveston Historical Foundation's Preservation Resource Center.)

In 1917, Pres. Woodrow Wilson was reluctant to get involved in World War I. When Germany sank the British passenger liner *Lusitania* in 1915 with American citizens aboard, Wilson remained neutral. When US commercial shipping was threatened, however, the president and Congress declared war on Germany on April 6, 1917. Wilson, who needed support for joining the war, authorized "The Four-Minute Men," volunteers to give four-minute speeches at theaters and local gatherings. In Galveston, six African American men volunteered for the unit. Shown here are, from left to right, (first row) H.T. Davis, Father J.W. Kerwin, and J.R. Gibson; (second row) J.T. Maxey, M.H. Montgomery, Dr. R.H. Stanton, and Theodore W. Patrick. Kerwin, a Catholic priest, chaired the Galveston unit. (Courtesy of the Rufus H. Stanton Jr. family.)

Two

ACTIVISTS AND POLITICIANS

Norris Wright Cuney was born near Hempstead, Texas, in 1846 to a prominent white plantation owner and a slave mother. At the age of 13, Cuney's father sent him to a school for blacks in Pennsylvania. During the Civil War, with his education interrupted, Cuney traveled around the United States for several years, eventually settling in Galveston, where he studied law and became a well-known figure in Texas and at the national level. During his life, Cuney served as city alderman and was appointed a school director of Galveston County. He was the first grand master of the Prince Hall Masons in Texas, from 1875 to 1877. In 1882, Cuney became special inspector of customs at Galveston and, eventually, collector of customs for the port in 1889. (Courtesy of Old Central Cultural Center Inc.)

As an activist, politician, and union leader, Cuney improved education for African Americans in Galveston and established a union for Galveston's black dockworkers. In 1879, Cuney was asked to lead the newly formed Cotton Jammers Association, a group of African American longshoremen who had been denied entry into the Screwmen's Benevolent Association. This group was made up of specialized longshoremen, who, with the aid of a tool called a screwjack, packed cotton into the holds of ships. (Courtesy of Galveston Historical Foundation's Preservation Resource Center.)

By 1882, Cuney was still unable to secure stevedoring contracts for the black longshoremen, despite labor shortages in peak seasons. To break the white longshoremen's monopoly on the wharves, Cuney brought a large number of black longshoremen from New Orleans in 1883. This gave him the workforce necessary to gain the stevedoring contract from Morgan Lines, one of the port's largest cotton shippers. (Courtesy of New York Public Library.)

In March 1883, Cuney organized the Screwmen's Benevolent Association No. 2. The president of the Galveston Cotton Exchange was informed that Cuney had both tools and an ample workforce. Their first job, on the ship *Albion*, resulted in an immediate withdrawal of all white workers, who called a strike. The white workers were brought back, but it was not an overwhelming victory for the black workers, as Cuney was still the only employer who hired the black workers throughout the 1880s and 1890s. (Courtesy of Galveston Historical Foundation's Preservation Resource Center.)

The introduction of the cotton compress in 1910 ended the need for all screwmen, both black and white, with both groups' associations forming affiliations with the national longshoremen's union. In 1983, on orders from a federal judge, the black chapters of the International Longshoremen Association (ILA), Local 851 and 329, were merged with the white ILA Local 307 and Hispanic ILA Local 1576 to form the present ILA Local 20. (Courtesy of Old Central Cultural Center Inc.)

Cuney held several positions with the Republican Party, including secretary of the state executive committee, first assistant to the sergeant-at-arms of the 12th state legislature, and, eventually, chairman of the Texas Republican Party, where he became a national committeeman. He was a delegate to the Republican National Conventions from 1872 to 1892 and ran for mayor of Galveston and the state senate, but was defeated in both elections. His role with the Republican Party presented opportunities for improving the lives of African Americans in Galveston and Texas. Today, the Wright Cuney Recreational Center at 718 Forty-first Street honors his memory. (Photograph by David Canright; courtesy of Galveston Historical Foundation.)

Leroy G. Hoskins Jr. was born in Burleson County, Texas, and moved to Galveston as a young man seeking employment. He found work with the International Longshoreman's Association, Local No. 851, in 1945. During his employment, he held several positions, including financial secretary, member of the board of directors, and assistant business agent. He was elected president in 1966. Hoskins was successful in negotiating consistent employment for African American workers. A civil rights leader, he spoke on behalf of the underserved. At a time when paying a poll tax was required to vote, Hoskins found ways to raise money for those who needed assistance. He was an active board member of the United Way, YMCA, Boy Scouts of America, Yeager Home for Children, Galveston Housing Authority, Big Brothers Big Sisters, St. Mary's Hospital, the Downtown Rotary Club, Coalition of Black Democrats, and NAACP. (Courtesy of the Leroy G. Hoskins Jr. family.)

Born and raised in Galveston, Eldrewey Stearns is considered the first civil rights leader in Houston. Stopped by Houston police one night in 1959 for having defective taillights, Stearns was arrested and beaten for having a picture of a white girl in his wallet. At the time, he was a law student at Texas Southern University in Houston. After the incident, he encouraged students to join him in a lunch counter sit-in. Stearns's integration effort was successful, and other protest activities slowly and quietly integrated Houston. (Courtesy of Old Central Cultural Center Inc.)

Louisiana native Thomas D. Armstrong was a teacher in Port Arthur and Louisiana before moving to Galveston in 1938, where he became one of the most successful African American businessmen of the time. In 1948, Armstrong (center) and Mack Hannah (left) became the first black delegates from Texas to attend the Democratic National Convention. In 1961, Armstrong was the first African American elected to Galveston's city council, and was a delegate to the Democratic conventions in 1964 and 1968. (Courtesy of Rosenberg Library, Galveston.)

As a senior at Central High School, Kelton Sams was a leading civil rights activist, organizing Galveston's department store lunchroom sit-ins in 1961. Within a few months, all segregated restaurants, coffee shops, and other businesses served African Americans. (Courtesy of Rosenberg Library, Galveston.)

Delta Sigma Theta Sorority was founded on January 13, 1913, at Howard University in Washington, DC. Galvestonian Jessie McGuire Dent, a founding member, served as secretary of the newly formed sorority. The sorority participated in the March 3, 1913, Women's Suffrage Parade and was the only African American women's organization in attendance. The march was the sorority's first act of social advocacy for the 22 founding members. (Courtesy of Old Central Cultural Center Inc.)

Thomas D. Armstrong, or "TD," was considered one of Galveston's most successful African American business leaders. He was often referred to as one of Texas's few "negro millionaires." Armstrong's business accomplishments included the Armstrong-Strode Funeral Home, Armstrong Drug Store, the BA&P Realty Company, T.D. Armstrong Realty, T.D.A. Investment Company, the Little Shamrock Motel & Coffee Shop, and the Tyler Life Insurance Company. The latter became one of the largest Texas-owned, predominantly African American insurance companies in the state. (Courtesy of Old Central Cultural Center Inc.)

Three

ENTREPRENEURS

Hazel Davis, born in New Orleans in 1905, became a beautician at the age of 16. She moved to Galveston and married Leon Phillips Sr. in 1937. That same year, Hazel became the first African American female to have a licensed beauty shop in Galveston. (Courtesy of Leon Phillips Jr.)

Mr. and Mrs. Albertine Yeager moved to Galveston and opened a nursery and Kindergarten in their home. Mrs. Yeager's Kindergarten, begun during World War I, allowed mothers who needed to work to have a place for their children to be cared for. By 1930, the nursery and Kindergarten became a nonprofit orphanage; daily attendance reached 108 children by 1931. (Courtesy of Rosenberg Library, Galveston.)

Gus Allen (far right) is pictured visiting Honey Brown's Barbeque Cafe. Honey Brown, or "Honey" as he was called, is standing at the end of the counter, to the left of Allen. (Courtesy of Rosenberg Library, Galveston.)

Astute businessman Gus Allen opened several businesses on Seawall Boulevard and Twenty-eighth Street, as most of the beachfront activities for African Americans were confined to this one-block area. Within that block, Allen owned and operated Gus Allen's Café (shown here), the Jambalaya Restaurant, and Gus Allen's Hotel. (Courtesy of Rosenberg Library, Galveston.)

Also located in the 2800 block of Seawall Boulevard was Gus Allen's Hotel. Although African American activities were limited to a one-block area, many great memories were formed by people who came to visit from all over the country. This photograph of Allen (seated, third from left) and his staff was taken by Charles Manney of Chicago. (Courtesy of Rosenberg Library, Galveston.)

In the early 1930s,
Gus Allen opened
the Dreamland Café,
located at 2704 Church
Street. The business
lasted several years
before closing in the
late 1940s. In 1980, the
building was demolished.
(Courtesy of Galveston
Historical Foundation's
Preservation
Resource Center.)

In 1939, B.M. Jackson
became one of the first
African American
publishers and editors for
the *Galveston Examiner*
newspaper. (Courtesy of
Houston Metropolitan
Research Center,
Houston Public Library.)

Thomas Green (1912–1995) was the owner of Green's Funeral Home, catering to the African American community. A licensed real estate broker and licensed bail bondsman, Green also operated Green's Bonding Service. During his lifetime, he served on the board of directors for many organizations throughout Galveston County. (Courtesy of Center for 20th Century Texas Studies.)

Selena Fulton opened Selena's Blue Room in 1944 in a remodeled carport behind the Jones Grocery at Thirty-third and Ball Streets. She later took over the old grocery store, remodeling it with mirrors and 100 blue Naugahyde chairs. The Blue Room was host to some of the top names in the entertainment world, including T-Bone Walker and Little Esther Phillips. During Galveston's "Open City" era, Selena's was open 24 hours a day and was a favorite breakfast spot and watering hole for many African American longshoremen and railroad workers. (Courtesy of Leon Banks Jr.)

Top acts from all over the nation, including T-Bone Walker, Dina Washington, and Little Esther Phillips, would come to Selena's Blue Room after they finished their shows at the Galveston City Auditorium (since demolished). Drink specials included Falstaff and Jax beer for 15¢ a bottle, attracting customers of all colors long before integration. The club was a jumping-off point for many local musicians, including jazz drummer G.T. Hogan. (Photograph by David Canright; courtesy of Galveston Historical Foundation.)

Born in Galveston, Anna Dupree moved to Houston in 1916, supporting herself as a maid and housekeeper for white families while she worked her way through beauty school. She became a prominent businesswoman, opening hair salons throughout the Houston area. In 1952, she opened the Eliza Johnson Home for Aged Negroes on a 35-acre tract in the African American community of Sunnyside. Although five facilities for the aged were already operating in Houston at the time, none admitted African Americans. (Courtesy of the Houston Metropolitan Research Center, Houston Public Library.)

The Busy Bee Taxi Company was the first taxi service in Galveston that catered to the African American community. The hub of its operation was located on Twenty-sixth Street, between Church and Post Office Streets. (Courtesy of Rosenberg Library, Galveston.)

Standard Cleaners and Dyers, a dry cleaners catering to the African American community, occupied this building at 410 Twenty-sixth Street. Owned by James Lockett, the operation opened in the 1930s and lasted until the end of the 1940s. The building was demolished in the 1980s. (Courtesy of Galveston Historical Foundation's Preservation Resource Center.)

Ira Captain owned and operated the Big Tree Café, at 2702 Post Office Street. The café served the African American community during the 1940s. The building was demolished in the 1980s. (Courtesy of Galveston Historical Foundation's Preservation Resource Center.)

In 1906, Fellman's Dry Goods Store relocated from Market Street to a new building at 2202–2204 Post Office Street. The company was one of the first retail establishments to hire African American women to work in their waiting rooms. As a result, the store had the highest African American trade in Galveston. (Courtesy of Galveston Historical Foundation's Preservation Resource Center.)

The Savoy Beauty Salon, managed and operated by Laura Mae O'Neal (far left), was located at 2710 Church Street. The salon catered to African American women and girls from the 1940s to 1985. It was yet another business enterprise of Galveston entrepreneur Gus Allen. (Courtesy of David O'Neal.)

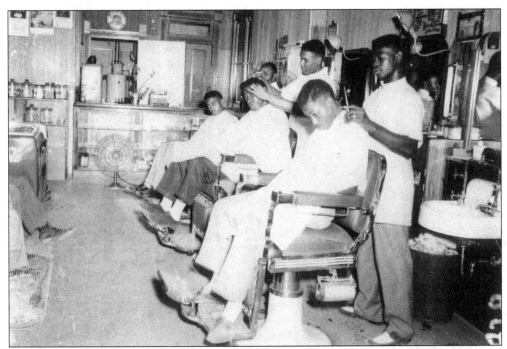

During the 1960s, Sellers Barber Shop was owned and operated by Eldridge Sellers Jr. It was located at 3413 Ball Street, where Sellers also operated a small hotel. (Courtesy of Rosenberg Library, Galveston.)

African American teachers employed with Galveston Independent School District opened a separate credit union for themselves in 1951, because they were declined membership in the district's all-white credit union. In 1955, they opened enrollment to district employees of all colors. A portable building behind the campus of Alamo Elementary School, at Fifty-third Street and Avenue N 1/2, served as the union's office. Still in operation today, the office is now located inside the main Alamo building. (Photograph by David Canright; courtesy of Galveston Historical Foundation.)

Founded in 1840 by Rev. James Huskins as an outgrowth for the slaves belonging to the congregation of First Baptist Church, Avenue L Baptist Church is the oldest African American Baptist church in the state of Texas. In 1855, First Baptist Church leaders purchased land from the city, and the slave congregation moved to the Avenue L site (2612 Avenue L) with Rev. Israel S. Campbell serving as pastor. Following the Civil War, the church was deeded to their congregation. The original building was destroyed by the 1900 hurricane. Tanner Brother's Contractors and Architects, an African American firm, constructed the current church in 1916. A part of the 1904 wood sanctuary is visible today from the west side. Since the 1840s, members of Avenue L Baptist Church have made significant contributions to the community of Galveston. (Photograph by David Canright; courtesy of Galveston Historical Foundation.)

Four

SACRED PLACES

The 1900 storm severely damaged the original Avenue L church building, leaving only the front facade standing. (Courtesy of Galveston County Museum.)

West Point Missionary Baptist Church was organized in 1870 as West Point Free Mission Baptist Church. Rev. E.T. Hall served as the pastor. The current building, at 3009 Avenue M, was completed in 1921 with funds donated by African American longshoremen. (Photograph by David Canright; courtesy of Galveston Historical Foundation.)

A young West Point Baptist Church member, Johnnie Quinine Jr., is pictured dressed for Sunday school. He is posing in front of his home at the Bayview Apartments in the 3000 block of Market Street (Avenue D), where he lived with his parents, Johnnie and Thelma. From 1945 until 1976, West Point was ministered by Rev. Jefferson F. Sargent. He and his wife, Sister Lola, conducted Bible schools and symposia during the summer months, in addition to the regular Bible studies every Sunday. (Courtesy of Johnnie Quinine family.)

First Union Baptist Church was founded in 1870 as the First Union Free Missionary Baptist Church, organized by a delegation representing the American Baptist Free Mission Society of Boston, an interracial antislavery group. First Union was the first church in Texas organized by the group and was known as the mother church of the Texas State Convention. (Courtesy of Galveston Historical Foundation Preservation Resource Center.)

In 1955, the congregation of First Union Baptist Church posed in front of their new building. The church pastor that year was Rev. J.I. Jackson. (Courtesy First Union Baptist Church Archives.)

Members of the Interdenominational Ministerial Alliance are seen in this composite photograph from 1933. (Courtesy of First Union Baptist Church Archives.)

Mount Olive Missionary Baptist Church was organized in 1876 as an extension of Avenue L Missionary Baptist Church, to serve African Americans who lived in the western part of the city. Rev. D.H. Shivers was appointed the temporary pastor. The original building was destroyed by the 1900 storm and rebuilt under the guidance of Rev. E.M. Wright. The current church at 3602 Sealy (Avenue I) was built in 1969, under the leadership of Rev. M.C. Battle. (Courtesy of Galveston Historical Foundation's Preservation Resource Center.)

In this early 1920s photograph, Mount Olive member Cornelius Alfred Harris sits behind the wheel of his car, which is parked in front of the church. (Courtesy of Cornelia Harris-Banks.)

Mount Pilgrim Missionary Baptist Church was organized in 1883 on the corner of Thirtieth Street and Avenue I. Originally called West Mount Pilgrim Baptist Church, the growing congregation purchased property at Thirty-second Street and Broadway, where the current building was erected. (Photograph by David Canright; courtesy of Galveston Historical Foundation.)

Saint Luke Missionary Baptist Church organized in 1894 with 36 members from First Union Missionary Baptist. They met in homes until a lot with two houses was obtained at Fifteenth Street and Avenue N. After those structures were destroyed in the 1900 hurricane, the congregation moved to a building at Ninth Street and Broadway, then to the present site at 1301 Avenue L in 1911. (Courtesy of Galveston Historical Foundation's Preservation Resource Center.)

Macedonia Missionary Baptist Church was organized in 1889 by a group that realized the need for more churches in the African American community. The congregation worshipped in a building near the beach before securing the location at Avenue M and Twenty-ninth Street. The structure was subsequently damaged by the 1900 hurricane. The present building (shown here) was erected in its place. (Photograph by David Canright; courtesy of Galveston Historical Foundation.)

Trinity Missionary Baptist Church at 1223 Thirty-second Street was another extension of Avenue L Baptist Church. Organized in the 1890s, it is known today as Bible Way Baptist Church. (Photograph by David Canright; courtesy of Galveston Historical Foundation.)

Reedy Chapel African Methodist Church was Texas's first African American Episcopal Church, established in 1848 by the members of the Methodist Episcopal Church South as a place for their congregation's slaves to worship. A fire destroyed the church in 1885. The following year, the church was reorganized. A new building was completed in 1888 and immediately turned over to the freed slaves. Located at 2013 Broadway, the building's masonry work was done by church member Norris Wright Cuney. (Courtesy of Galveston Historical Foundation's Preservation Resource Center.)

More than 30 ministers have served the congregation at Reedy Chapel, including Bishop Josiah Haynes Armstrong. Born in Pennsylvania in 1842, Armstrong was a veteran of the Civil War, having fought with the US Colored Infantry. He entered the church in Florida in 1868, under Rev. William Bradwell. Armstrong was ordained a deacon in 1869, became an elder in 1870, and was ordained a bishop in 1896. He died in Galveston in 1898 and is buried in Lakeview Cemetery. (Above, courtesy of Galveston Historical Foundation's Preservation Resource Center; right, courtesy of State Archives of Florida, *Florida Memory*, http://floridamemory.com/items/show/137204.)

Saint Paul United Methodist Church was organized in 1866 through a division of parishioners from Reedy Chapel. The congregation purchased land in the 800 block of Ball Street (Avenue H) and began services under the direction of Rev. Samuel Osborn. In 1902, the congregation sold its property on Ball Street and purchased land on the southeast corner of Broadway and Thirteenth Street, where it worships today. (Courtesy of Galveston Historical Foundation's Preservation Resource Center.)

Wesley Tabernacle United Methodist Church emerged from the congregation of Saint Paul's. Rev. Peter Cavanaugh organized the church in 1869 in a one-room house on Broadway, between Thirty-eighth and Thirty-ninth Streets. As the church grew, the present location on Twenty-eighth Street and Sealy (Avenue I) was purchased, and the one-room house was moved. After a fire and the 1900 hurricane damaged the house, a new one-story building was constructed. In 1924, the church was remodeled by raising the building and constructing a new first floor. (Courtesy of Galveston Historical Foundation's Preservation Resource Center.)

Rev. Perrie Joy Jackson was the valedictorian for Central High School's graduating class in 1953. She served as a pastor in Hitchcock, Texas City, and Galveston, and was a former educator. She was the first African American woman to earn a master's degree in the field of sacred theology from Southern Methodist University and, in 1962, was the first African American woman ordained into the Texas Conference of Methodist Churches. Jackson founded the First United Methodist Church in Prairie View, Texas, and was a lifelong member of Galveston's Wesley Tabernacle, serving 43 years as its pastor. She was also a Golden Life Member of Delta Sigma Theta Sorority. (Courtesy of the Reverend Perrie Joy Jackson family.)

Shiloh African Methodist Episcopal Church was organized in 1870 after the Methodist Episcopal bishop was notified that a church was needed for people who resided west of Twenty-fifth Street. Land was purchased at 1310 Twenty-ninth Street. The original buildings were destroyed by hurricanes in 1894 and in 1900. The present structure was erected in 1923. In 1971, Shiloh became the first African American church in Texas to receive a state historical marker. (Photograph by David Canright; courtesy of Galveston Historical Foundation.)

Saint Augustine of Hippo Episcopal Church is the oldest African American parish in the Episcopal Diocese of Texas. It was organized in 1884 to minister to black Anglicans from the British West Indies. The church was originally located on Broadway and Twenty-second Street. It was moved to its current location in 1940. (Photograph by David Canright; courtesy of Galveston Historical Foundation.)

Holy Rosary Catholic Church is the first African American Catholic church in the state of Texas. It was organized in 1889, with Father Philip Keller, a native of Germany, acting as the first resident priest for the parish. Originally located on Avenue L and Twenty-fifth Street, the parish moved to its current location at Thirty-first and Avenue N in 1914. (Courtesy of Galveston Historical Foundation's Preservation Resource Center.)

Two young members of Holy Rosary receive their first communion in 1920. (Courtesy of the Charles and Anita Jones family.)

William Hebert established the W.K. Hebert Funeral Home in 1919 at 2827 Avenue M 1/2, after ending his partnership with Columbus Willis and their business, Willis & Hebert Undertakers and Embalmers. The W.K. Hebert Funeral Home was family owned and operated until 1988. (Photograph by David Canright; courtesy of Galveston Historical Foundation.)

Field's Funeral Home was established in 1949 by Willie Fields and his wife, Geneva. The couple also owned and operated a grocery and market on Forty-fourth Street. The funeral home remains in operation today. (Photograph by David Canright; courtesy of Galveston Historical Foundation.)

In 1911, a group of African American citizens formed the Rosewood Cemetery Association, purchasing an eight-acre tract of land on Seawall Boulevard between Sixty-first and Sixty-third Streets. Individuals, churches, and African American organizations purchased shares in the association. Burial plots were sold for $10, with an additional $2 for grave digging. Prior to the establishment of Rosewood, African American citizens were prohibited from interring their dead in most of the city's cemeteries. The first interment was Robert Bailey, an infant who died in February 1912. The last known burial was Frank Boyer, in June 1944. Records list over 400 graves in Rosewood, although markers currently exist for only 20. (Photograph by David Canright; courtesy of Galveston Historical Foundation.)

In 1947, Thomas "TD" Armstrong purchased the remaining shares from the Rosewood Association. The city began purchasing undeveloped portions of the cemetery in 1951, and by the late 1950s, the remaining land was gradually sold off to developers. After Armstrong's death in 1972, his estate sold the cemetery to John Saracco, who donated the cemetery to Galveston Historical Foundation in 2006 in an effort to preserve what remains of the historic site. (Photograph by David Canright; courtesy of Galveston Historical Foundation.)

With funds made available from the Freedmen's Bureau, white missionary Sarah Barnes established the Barnes Institute in 1869. This was the first school for African Americans in Galveston. The school was located on Avenue M between Twenty-eighth and Twenty-ninth Streets. John Ogilvie Stevenson, a native of Scotland, served with the American Missionary Association and was the school's first principal. By 1876, the campus had four teachers and an enrollment of more than 300 students. Frank Webb became principal in 1881, serving until 1894. During his time, the school grew significantly and was renamed the West District Colored School. (Courtesy of Rosenberg Library, Galveston.)

Five

INSTITUTES OF LEARNING

The West District School, located on Winnie Street (Avenue G) between Twenty-seventh and Twenty-eighth Streets, was an elementary school for African American children who lived west of Twentieth Street. By 1890, the school had relocated to the south side of Avenue M, between Twenty-eighth and Twenty-ninth Streets. (Courtesy of Rosenberg Library, Galveston.)

A second elementary school for African American children living east of Twenty-fifth Street was established in 1871. The East District School was located on the north side of Avenue J (Broadway) between Ninth and Tenth Streets. (Courtesy of Rosenberg Library, Galveston.)

Viola Scull (Fedford), a teacher at West District School, is pictured here with her class in 1910. (Courtesy of Rosenberg Library, Galveston.)

The faculty of the West District School posed for a photograph on May 31, 1935. H.T. Davis was the principal of the campus that year. (Courtesy of Rosenberg Library, Galveston.)

Boy Scouts raise the American flag at George W. Carver Elementary School in the 1950s. This school, formerly the West District School, was located at 1410 Thirty-seventh Street. (Courtesy of Rosenberg Library, Galveston.)

Cornelius Harris (far right), principal of Booker T. Washington Elementary School in the 1960s, entertained the faculty at his home. (Courtesy of Cornelia Harris Banks.)

A Central High School homecoming float passes Booker T. Washington Elementary School in the 1950s. The school's name was changed from the East District School in 1939. It was located at Twenty-seventh Street and Avenue M. (Courtesy of Old Central Cultural Center Inc.)

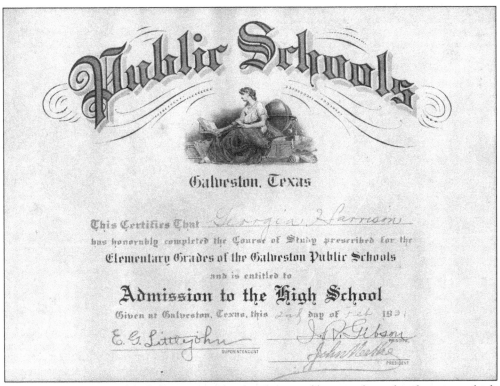

Georgia Harrison completed elementary school and received her certificate for admission to high school on February 2, 1931. (Courtesy of Sherman Batiste Boyer.)

Private Kindergarten teacher Miss Edna Brown poses with her class in 1938. The Galveston City Directory that year noted two public schools for African American students: George Washington Carver Elementary and Central High School, with several private schools for African Americans also available. (Courtesy of Old Central Cultural Center Inc.)

Organized in 1885, Galveston's Central High School was the first high school for African Americans in Texas. Its first classrooms were housed in a rented building located at Sixteenth Street and Avenue L. (Courtesy of Old Central Cultural Central Inc.)

Central High School's second location also was in a rented building. Between 1886 and 1893, the school operated from its location at Fifteenth Street and Avenue N. (Courtesy of Old Central Cultural Center Inc.)

In 1893, land was purchased between Twenty-sixth and Twenty-seventh Streets on Avenue M for a new school, designed by the notable Galveston architect Nicholas Clayton. The handsome brick structure was the third campus for Central High School. (Courtesy of Galveston Historical Foundation's Preservation Resource Center.)

In 1924, a new wing was added to the west side of the 1893 building in order to increase the number of classrooms available for the growing enrollment. (Courtesy of Old Central Cultural Central Inc.)

From the collaboration of the all-white Rosenberg Library Association, the Galveston School Board, and the city of Galveston, the school board authorized the addition of a public library to Central High School on May 18, 1904. The Colored Branch of the Rosenberg Library became a reality on January 11, 1905. It was the first African American public library in Texas. (Photograph by David Canright; courtesy of Galveston Historical Foundation.)

Upon graduating from Central High School in 1916, Lillian Josephine Davis started her career working as an assistant in the school's library. She worked under three Central High principals. At that time, the principal supervised the library. When L.A. Morgan became principal in 1941, he gave Davis the official title of librarian. (Courtesy of Old Central Cultural Center Inc.)

This very rare photograph shows students checking out books from the Colored Branch of Rosenberg Library. (Courtesy of Old Central Cultural Center Inc.)

Central High School's first band poses for a group photograph on the steps of the school in 1915. (Courtesy of Rosenberg Library, Galveston.)

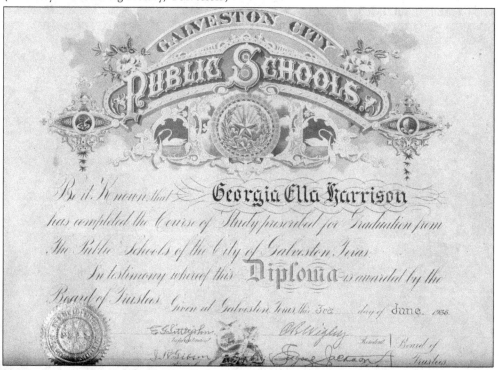

Shown here is Georgia Ella Harrison's diploma from Central High School, dated June 3, 1935. (Courtesy of Sherman Batiste Boyer.)

The final Central High School, built in 1954, stretched from Thirty-first to Thirty-third Streets between Avenues H and I. (Courtesy of Old Central Cultural Center Inc.)

Dedication
Former Principals of Central
High School

J. R. GIBSON
1886-1936

W. J. MASON
1936-1941

DR. L. A. MORGAN
1941-1967

This page from a 1960s Central High School yearbook honors the institution's past principals. J.R. Gibson was the first principal, fulfilling the obligation for 50 years. He was succeeded by W.J. Mason, who served as principal from 1936 until 1941. Dr. L.A. Morgan held the post from 1941 until 1967. (Courtesy of Old Central Cultural Center Inc.)

Frank Window served as assistant principal at Central High School from 1948 to 1968. (Courtesy of Old Central Cultural Center Inc.)

Lucy E. Jones taught language arts at Central High School in the 1940s and 1950s. (Courtesy of Houston Metropolitan Research Center, Houston Public Library.)

Central High School band member Edward Huff Jones poses in his uniform for his school photograph in the 1940s. (Courtesy of Houston Metropolitan Research Center, Houston Public Library.)

In 1962, Central High School's baseball team won the state championship. Coach Floyd Iglehart led the team to victory. (Courtesy of Old Central Cultural Center Inc.)

Central High School's football team won the 1964 state championship. (Courtesy of Old Central Cultural Center Inc.)

The coaches for Central High School's 1964 state championship football team pose for a photograph. From left to right are Kermit Courville, Leon Bedford, Edgar Collins, head coach Edward Mitchell, Ray Dohn Dillon, and Robert Campbell. (Courtesy of Old Central Cultural Center Inc.)

With the merging of the two Galveston public high schools, African American Central High School and Ball High School for white students, James Sweatt Jr. served as the last principal of Central High School for its last school year, 1967–1968. After the merger, Central High School became Central Middle School, and Ball High School became the only public high school in Galveston. (Courtesy of Old Central Cultural Center Inc.)

The senior class officers for the last graduating class of Central High School pose for their yearbook photograph. The academic year 1967–1968 was the last for the school. (Courtesy of Old Central Cultural Center Inc.)

Central High School

Alma Mater

*Central High Our
Alma Mater
We Will Cherish Thee
We Will Strive
To Keep
Thee Ever
In Our Memory*

*With The Blue
And
White Before Us
True Forever More
Till The End
of Time We'll
Fight For*

*Dear Old
Central High*

Shown here is Central High School's *Alma Mater*. The lyrics were written by Dr. L.A. Morgan, principal of Central High School from 1941 to 1967. (Courtesy of Old Central Cultural Center Inc.)

Shown here are, from left to right, Dr. E.M. Stanton, African American schools' physician (a clinic was located on the Central High School campus); Central High School head football coach and physical education department chair Ray T. Sheppard; and Dr. L.A. Morgan, principal of Central High School. (Courtesy of Rosenberg Library, Galveston.)

IN THE DISTRICT COURT OF THE UNITED STATES
FOR THE SOUTHERN DISTRICT OF TEXAS
GALVESTON DIVISION

JESSIE MCGUIRE DENT, ET AL)
)
            VS.   )
)   CIVIL ACTION NO. __227__
THE BOARD OF TRUSTEES OF THE   )
PUBLIC FREE SCHOOLS OF THE   )
CITY OF GALVESTON, TEXAS,   )
ET AL   )

FINAL JUDGMENT

        The Plaintiff, Jessie McGuire Dent, individually and
on behalf of others similarly situated, filed her complaint herein
on the 15th day of June, 1943, and the defendants filed their answer
on the 15th day of June, 1943; and, both the plaintiff and defendants
appeared by their respective attorneys on said date and submitted
this cause on the complaint and answer filed.

        WHEREUPON, plaintiff, by her attorney, moved the court
for a summary judgment on the pleadings on the grounds that there
is now no genuine issue as to any material fact and that plaintiff
is entitled to a judgment as a matter of law, the plaintiff, by her
attorney, and the defendants, by their attorneys, hereby consent to
the entering of the final judgment herein;

        IT IS HEREBY ORDERED, DECREED AND ADJUDGED as follows:
That this Court has jurisdiction of the subject matter and all the
persons and parties hereto; that the complaint states a cause of
action against the defendants under Section 24 (14) of the Judicial
Code (28 U. S. Code, Section 41 (14) and under Section 43 of Title
8 of the U. S. Code.

        Pursuant to Section 247 (d) of the Judicial Code (28)
U. S. Code, Section 400), it is DELCARED AND ADJUDGED:

        That the official policy and official acts of the
defendants, The Board of Trustees of the Public Free Schools of
the City of Galveston, Texas, and S. B. Graham, Superintendent of
the Public Schools of the City of Galveston, in carrying out the
custom and practice that has been in existence for many years of
paying the plaintiff and all other Negro teachers, dean, secretaries
and principals in the Public School System of Galveston, Texas,
smaller salaries than are paid by said defendants to white teachers,
deans, secretaries and principals, with the same professional quali-
fications and experience, insofar as such differentials are predi-
cated on race or color, are unlawful and unconstitutional, and are
in violation of the equal protection clause of the Fourteenth
Amendment of the Constitution of the United States and of Section 41
of Title 8 of the United States Code:

Jessie McGuire Dent was hired to teach Latin at Central High School in 1913 and later became Central High School's dean of girls. In 1943, represented by attorney W.J. Durham of Sherman, Texas, Dent was the plaintiff in a lawsuit against Galveston Independent School District (GISD), seeking equal pay for African American GISD educators. On June 15, 1943, US Judge T.M. Kennerly ruled for the plaintiff. Judge Kennerly instructed the district, beginning in September 1943, to increase salaries of African American principals, deans, teachers, and secretaries over the next three years, to achieve complete equality by September 1945. (Courtesy of Galveston Independent School District.)

Joyce Ann Hunter (Daniel) was Central High School's "Miss Homecoming" for the 1957–1958 school year. (Courtesy of Joyce Ann Hunter Daniel.)

W.G. Dickerson (far left) sponsored the Central High School Clef Club, a traveling talent production, in the 1950s and 1960s. Dickerson was a social studies teacher who also sponsored the Central High Student Council. (Courtesy of Old Central Cultural Center Inc.)

The Aqua Velvets, members of the Central High School's Clef Club, rehearse in 1960. (Courtesy of Old Central Cultural Center Inc.)

Members of the Central High School National Honor Society pose in 1959. Spanish teacher Sarah L. Harris sponsored the group. (Courtesy of Old Central Cultural Center Inc.)

During the 1950s, Central High School's band (above) and Drum and Bugle Corps (below) were led by Fleming S. Huff. (Both courtesy of Old Central Cultural Center Inc.)

Central High School cheerleaders and mascots pose for a yearbook photograph in 1959. Health and physical education teachers Frankie B. Sheppard and Doris S. McNeill sponsored the group. (Courtesy of Old Central Cultural Center Inc.)

Central High School's Blue and White Battalion was sponsored by Frankie Sheppard and Doris McNeill in the 1950s. The team captain was Alretha Horne, with Jessie Curtis, Eddie Chapman, and Peggy Wyatt serving as lieutenants. (Courtesy of Old Central Cultural Center Inc.)

Theasel Henderson was the first African American to serve on the Galveston Independent School Board. During his tenure, from 1968 until 1986, Henderson served in several positions, including president. (Courtesy of Galveston Independent School District.)

Holy Rosary Parish established the first African American Catholic school in Texas in 1886, on the corner of Twelfth Street and Avenue K. To accommodate the increased enrollment, a new school was erected in 1888 at Twenty-fifth and Sealy (Avenue I). By 1898, the parish built and organized Holy Rosary Industrial School. This institution was intended to be a school of domestic arts as well as an orphanage for homeless girls. In 1914, the school buildings were moved to Avenue N, between Thirtieth and Thirty-first Streets (pictured). A high school curriculum was added in 1927, making it the first accredited Catholic high school for African Americans in the state of Texas. Financial problems closed the high school in 1941. A new convent and lower grade school were built in 1956 under the leadership of Father George Reynolds. One year later, parishioners witnessed the dedication of the new Holy Rosary School. Within 10 years, the buildings had been replaced by modern, fire-resistant structures. Later, a cafeteria, additional classrooms, an office, and a library were added to the parish school. Construction costs were covered by a generous gift from parishioner W.K. Herbert, a local funeral home owner. By the late 1960s, the school again faced financial problems, and by 1967, the seventh- and eighth-grade classes were dropped. Still facing financial problems, Holy Rosary School closed its doors on May 28, 1979. (Courtesy of Roberta "Cookie" Taylor.)

Holy Rosary Catholic School student Blanche Scarlet is pictured at her high school graduation in the late 1930s. (Courtesy of the Charles H. and Anita Jones family.)

Holy Rosary School graduates stop to pose during a ceremony in the 1960s. (Courtesy of the Charles H. and Anita Jones family.)

A rare 1900 photograph shows a nurse (second from right) with her young African American patients at what is labeled an "isolation unit." Before freedom arrived in Galveston on June 19, 1865, slaves needing medical attention were taken care of by their owners. After slavery, most African Americans received treatment in their homes or in segregated areas, called "colored wards," in hospitals. African American doctors could not practice in these wards, however. In 1903, Mary Susan Moore and her husband, James D. Moore, established the Hubbard Sanitarium. The facility functioned until the middle of the 1920s. Many other African American doctors also worked hard to bring equality to the medical profession. (Courtesy of Moody Medical Library, University of Texas Medical Branch, Galveston.)

Six

HEALTH AND WELLNESS

In August 1886, in the office of Galveston doctors J.H. and L.M. Wilkins, a meeting was called to order. Here, doctors from all across the state formed the Lone Star State Medical, Dental and Pharmaceutical Association. The association was the first African American medical association in the state of Texas and the second in the nation. Dr. Benjamin Jessie Covington (pictured) was born in Marlin, Texas, in 1869. The son of former slaves, Dr. Covington is credited as being one of the founders of the medical association. (Courtesy of Houston Metropolitan Research Center, Houston Public Library.)

Mary Madison, a free black nurse living in Galveston before the Civil War, was born in Virginia around 1820. She came to Galveston in 1841 and established a reputation as a "valuable citizen" administering health care to the community. In 1851, a petition (pictured) was sent to the Texas legislature on Madison's behalf, asking that she be able to stay in Galveston as a "free negro." The petition was in response to an 1840 Republic of Texas law that required free blacks to leave Texas or be sold into slavery. More than 80 white Galvestonians signed the petition, which was approved by the legislature that same year. (Courtesy Texas State Library, Austin, Archives Division.)

Dr. Joseph Mack Mosely Sr. (1899–1946) graduated from Meharry Medical College in Nashville, Tennessee, in 1913. He opened his first medical practice in Galveston in 1916. His son, Dr. Joseph Mack Mosely III, later joined his father's practice. (Courtesy of the Dr. Rufus H. Stanton Jr. family.)

Rufus H. Stanton Sr. was the eldest of the Stanton brothers. He worked as a barber and a pharmacist before becoming a dentist. To pay his way through Meharry Medical College, the first medical college in the South to admit African Americans, Stanton worked as a Pullman porter on the railroads. Upon graduation from Meharry, Dr. Stanton opened his dental practice in Galveston in 1915. (Courtesy of the Dr. Rufus H. Stanton Jr. family.)

After graduating from Meharry Medical College, Dr. Robert T. Stanton returned to Galveston and practiced medicine the old-fashioned way, making house calls and delivering babies in the homes of his patients. He spoke Spanish fluently and delivered most of the Hispanic babies in Galveston during that time. He mixed many of his own medicines, dispensing them to his patients as needed. Dr. Stanton also invested in Galveston real estate and, at one time, owned the renowned Darragh house, which once stood on the corner of Church Street (Avenue F) and Fifteenth Street. (Courtesy of the Dr. Rufus H. Stanton Jr. family.)

Reapher Stanton, RPh, was the pharmacist at the Island City Drug Store on Post Office (Avenue E) and Twenty-eighth Streets. The drugstore was owned and operated by Reapher's father, Sandy Hezekiah Stanton. (Courtesy of the Dr. Rufus H. Stanton Jr. family.)

Dr. Elbert Stanton attended both Wiley College in Marshall, Texas, and Meharry Medical College. After graduation from Meharry in the 1930s, he returned to Galveston and joined his brother's medical practice. During his years of practice, he served as the physician for the Galveston Independent School District "Negro" schools. Elbert was active in politics, running for various political offices more than once. He was also a 32nd degree Freemason and served as potentate of the organization for many years. (Courtesy of the Dr. Rufus H. Stanton Jr. family.)

Seen in this 1965 photograph are, from left to right, Dr. Elbert Stanton, Galveston Independent School District "Negro" school physician; Dr. Leroy Sterling, Galveston Independent School District "Negro" school dentist; and Corine Prader, Central High School nurse. (Courtesy of Old Central Cultural Center Inc.)

Dr. Rufus "Billy" Stanton Jr. graduated from Wiley College and received his doctorate of dental science from Meharry Medical College. In 1953, he joined his uncles, Drs. Elbert and Robert Stanton, in their office before opening his own practice. Dr. Stanton practiced dentistry for over 40 years. He served on the United States Bank board of directors; the board of directors for St. Vincent's House, a charitable organization serving the disadvantaged and poor of Galveston County; and the city charter review board. (Courtesy of the Dr. Rufus H. Stanton Jr. family.)

In the early 20th century, because of the poor health conditions of many black Americans at that time, a national movement developed called Health Improvement Week. This later evolved into National Negro Health Week, which was observed annually from 1915 until 1951. Galveston teacher John. H. Clouser was instrumental in bringing the event to the Galveston schools, sponsoring it as the chairman of the Volunteer Health League. A Galveston street, J.H. Clouser Lane, honors his memory today. (Courtesy of Rosenberg Library, Galveston.)

During health week, posters, flyers, bulletins, and programs focusing on community health were distributed in the African American schools. The pastors of community churches gave "health sermons" and allowed congregants who worked in the medical community to make presentations. The week culminated with a parade through the African American part of town, west of Twenty-fifth Street. The parade terminated at a city park, where a picnic and concert would be presented. This rare 1938 photograph depicts African American students parading north on Twenty-sixth Street. (Courtesy of Rosenberg Library, Galveston.)

Galveston businessman Thomas "TD" Armstrong (behind the wheel) sponsored a float in the National Negro Health Week parade of 1950. The week's theme that year was "keys to health." (Courtesy of Old Central Cultural Center Inc.)

Herman Aladdin Barnett broke the color barrier in 1949 when he became the first African American to be admitted to the University of Texas Medical School in Galveston and, later, the first native African American Texan to graduate from a Texas medical college and to be licensed to practice medicine in the state. Born in Austin in 1926, Dr. Barnett is seen here as a child, standing with his parents, Herman Jr. and Lula. (Courtesy of Moody Medical Library, University of Texas Medical Branch, Galveston.)

The University of Texas
Medical Branch
Galveston, Texas

This is to Certify that

Herman A. Barnett, M. D.
Has Creditably Completed

Rotating Internship
July 1, 1953 to June 30, 1954

in the **John Sealy and Affiliated Hospitals**

Given under our hands at Galveston, Texas   this 30th day of June, 1954

_____
VICE PRESIDENT OF MEDICAL BRANCH

_____
MEDICAL DIRECTOR OF HOSPITALS

Dr. Barnett graduated with honors from the University of Texas Medical School in 1954. (Courtesy of Moody Medical Library, University of Texas Medical Branch, Galveston.)

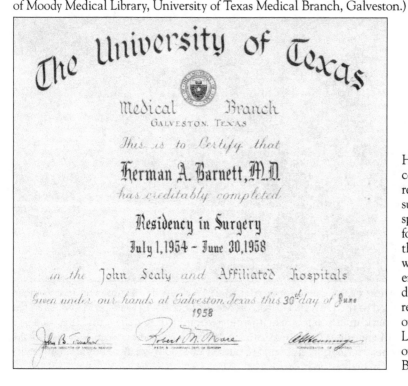

Herman Barnett completed his residency in surgery in 1958. He specialized in trauma, focusing on how the body changed when experiencing emergencies and during postoperative recoveries. (Courtesy of Moody Medical Library, University of Texas Medical Branch, Galveston.)

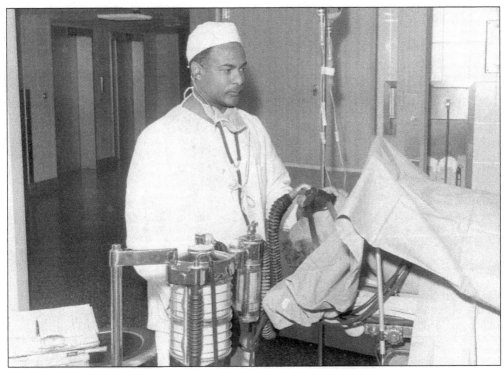

In 1968, Dr. Barnett completed his second residency at St. Joseph's Hospital in Houston. During his lifetime, he was affiliated with numerous hospitals, including the University of Texas Medical Branch (UTMB) Galveston hospitals, the Galveston County Memorial Hospital, and Hermann Hospital in Houston. (Courtesy of Moody Medical Library, University of Texas Medical Branch, Galveston.)

In 1973, Dr. Barnett was killed in an airplane crash. In his honor, friends and colleagues established the Herman A. Barnett Award, given annually to outstanding UTMB medical students since 1974. In 1978, Dr. Barnett posthumously received the Ashbel Smith Award, the University of Texas Medical Branch at Galveston's highest honor. (Courtesy of Melvin Williams.)

In 1902, the medical department of the University of Texas at Galveston built the first hospital for African Americans. The building was paid for through a $15,000 anonymous donation from a New York philanthropist and $35,000 from the 1900 Storm Central Relief Committee. (Courtesy of Moody Medical Library, University of Texas Medical Branch, Galveston.)

After World War I, the population of the city of Galveston increased, putting a strain on the capacity of the existing hospitals. A second hospital for African Americans (pictured) was opened on August 31, 1937. The cost of the building was $285,000. (Courtesy of Moody Medical Library, University of Texas Medical Branch, Galveston.)

Wilina Garner Mitchell Gatson, RN, BSN, was an honor graduate from Galveston's Central High School. Her drive to achieve and excel despite racial, gender, and cultural restrictions, led her to become a trailblazer in her field. She was the first African American female to graduate from the University of Texas Medical Branch bachelor of science nursing program, and she is a Distinguished Alumnus in the University of Texas Medical Branch Hall of Fame. (Courtesy of Alice Gatson.)

The Willing Workers Club, founded in 1923, was a charitable group of African American women from local churches who offered assistance to African American families in need by supplying various levels of support. The group held teas and other events to raise funds to help the less fortunate. (Courtesy of Sharon Batiste Boyer.)

Seven

CLUBS AND
ORGANIZATIONS

On December 5, 1935, Mary McLeod Bethune met with 37 women from across the country to share her vision of power and leadership through a national organization. Believing in the goodness of the human spirit and the capability of overcoming obstacles to reach a level of superior success, the organization she foresaw, the National Council of Negro Women, would be a networking facility advocating the use of collective power on issues concerning black women, family, and communities. In 1946, the Galveston chapter was formed and in 1948, Bethune (seated at center) led a meeting of the Galveston members at the Avenue L Baptist Church. (Courtesy of Rosenberg Library, Galveston.)

Members of the Adelphi Club pose in their formal attire in the 1960s. The club was founded in the 1940s to recognize outstanding young African American ladies in Galveston County. Their annual Debutante Ball was held during the holidays. A donated toy admitted the public to the club's annual toy dance. The toys were then distributed to Galveston County children. (Courtesy of Jeri Lyons.)

The Top Hat Men's Social and Charity Club was formed as a charitable organization to offer assistance and service in the community wherever they were needed. The club provided support to orphanages, St. Vincent's House, and other non-profit organizations. The group distributed Easter baskets to children and food baskets to needy families at Thanksgiving and Christmas. Their annual ball was always held during the winter holidays. (Courtesy of Lillie M. Little and James L.Brooks.)

Founded in the 1950s, the Sportsmen's Social and Charity Club was formed to assist African American families in the community. Among their contributions to the community were the donation of school supplies to children in need and scholarships to graduating African American male athletes. The group held an annual family picnic and an annual ball during the winter holidays. (Courtesy of Fred Turner.)

Another charitable men's organization that offered assistance to African American families in the community was the Diplomat Club, founded in the 1950s. The club owned its own clubhouse, located at 2601 Avenue K. The organization held several family events each year as well as an annual ball during the winter holidays. (Courtesy of Jeri Lyons and Janice Stanton.)

Alpha Kappa Alpha Sorority, the first national collegiate sorority for African American women, was founded in 1908 at Howard University, in Washington, DC, by nine young women. There, the club's motto, "Service to all Mankind," was adopted, along with its official colors, salmon pink and apple green. The Beta Phi Chapter was chartered in Galveston on March 23, 1938. Charter members were Ruby Bryant, Delle Curtis, Nellie Langston, Olivette Morgan, Bernice James, Lois Martin, E. Goldie Hunter, and Myrtle D. Thomas. During the early years of its existence, the sorority presented such luminaries as Jackie Robinson, Duke Ellington, and Etta Moten. Sorority activities include vocational guidance conferences, charity balls, school vaccination campaigns, and other programs to raise money for scholarships. (Courtesy of Beta Phi Omega Chapter, Alpha Kappa Alpha Sorority Inc. Archives.)

Delta Sigma Theta Sorority was founded in 1913 on the campus of Howard University in Washington, DC. Galveston's own Jessie McGuire Dent (seated, center) was one of the 22 founding members. Crimson and crème, denoting courage and purity, were selected as the colors. The Galveston alumnae chapter was chartered in 1941 as Gamma Delta and rechartered as the Galveston Alumnae Chapter in 1969. A public service sorority, the organization presents college scholarships to Galveston County high school seniors, monetary donations to nonprofit organizations that provide volunteers and assistance to the needy and offer programs on health concerns and voter education. Since the 1960s, the chapter has also honored African American couples married 50 years or more with teas and special luncheons. (Courtesy of Galveston Alumnae Chapter of Delta Sigma Theta Sorority Inc.)

Zeta Phi Beta Sorority was founded in 1920 through the persistence of Charles R.S. Taylor. His goal was to create a sorority that would be the sister organization to Phi Beta Sigma Fraternity. The sorority's colors of royal blue and white were accepted to match the colors of its brother fraternity. The Galveston chapter was chartered in 1942. Local programs include the signature Stork's Nest, the March of Dimes, Z-Hope, mentoring youth groups, Profiles of Women, and the Blue and White Cotillion. (Courtesy of Andrew Pierce III.)

Alpha Phi Alpha Fraternity was the first national collegiate fraternity for African American men. It was founded on the campus of Cornell University, in Ithaca, New York, on December 4, 1906. The chapter selected the motto "First of All, Servant of All, We Shall Transcend All." Black and gold were the colors chosen to represent the fraternity. The Galveston chapter was chartered in January 1942. Among the fraternity's annual projects are college scholarship awards, community science fairs, and voter registration drives. (Courtesy of Old Central Cultural Center Inc.)

Sigma Gamma Rho Sorority was founded in 1922 on the predominantly white campus of Butler University in Indianapolis, Indiana. Since its establishment, the organization has grown from a small, dedicated group of teachers to a vast national sorority with women from a variety of professional fields who continue to uphold the mission, "Great Service, Greater Progress." The local chapter, Alpha Thea Sigma, was chartered in Galveston in 1941. Projects include an annual Mother's Day brunch, symposia for young children, assistance for needy families, and college scholarship awards. (Courtesy of Marie Freeman.)

Kappa Alpha Psi Fraternity was founded at Indiana University in Bloomington in 1911. There were only 10 African American men on the campus at that time, but a vision existed to sow the seed of a fraternal tree. They selected the colors of crimson and crème. The Galveston chapter was chartered in 1950. Annual projects include donations to the Boy Scouts of America, work for Habitat for Humanity, voter registration drives, and college scholarships for high school seniors. (Courtesy of Old Central Cultural Center Inc.)

Galveston World War I soldier Charles H. Jones poses in his uniform. The Texas Naval Militia of Galveston was the first county unit to entrain for the war. Fort Crockett, on Seawall Boulevard, served as a US Army artillery training center for the troops bound for France. (Courtesy of Charles H. and Anita Jones.)

Eight

REMARKABLE GALVESTONIANS

Barry White (Barry Eugene Carter), the singer-songwriter, recorder, producer, arranger, and musician, was born in Galveston on September 12, 1944. Raised in California, he was introduced to music by his mother's classical record collection. His records became silver, gold, and platinum hits. White did voiceover work for several movies, television shows, and commercials. He also appeared as himself in television and movies. (Courtesy of Old Central Cultural Center Inc.)

D.H. "Doc" Hamilton held several positions with the International Longshoremen's Association Local No. 851, including president. Hamilton was the first African American to be elected to the executive board of the South Atlantic and Gulf Coast District of the International Longshoremen's Association. He died on August 5, 1939, and his funeral was held at Galveston's City Auditorium. (Courtesy of Galveston Historical Foundation.)

Married in 1958, Sterling and Freddie Patrick both graduated from Central High School. Sterling Phillips Patrick enrolled at Prairie View A&M, earning a bachelor's degree in education. He joined the Army and served in the Korean War from 1952 to 1955. He was honorably discharged as a first lieutenant. Sterling returned to Galveston and was hired to teach in the Galveston Independent School District. In 1967, the president of the United States appointed Sterling to Local Board No. 49 of the Selective Service System. He was the first African American in Galveston County appointed to this position. Freddie Gray Anderson Patrick attended Prairie View A&M after high school, but later enrolled in business school. Among other jobs, she worked as the secretary at Hendrick's Plumbing Company. In 1963, Freddie was the first African American hired in the city of Galveston's Water Department. (Courtesy of the Sterling and Freddie Patrick family.)

Little Esther Phillips (Esther Mae Jones) was born in Galveston on December 23, 1935. While a young child, her parents divorced and she divided her years between her father in Houston and her mother in Galveston. As a teenager, Esther moved to California with her mother and older sister. She was very talented and was raised singing in church. Shortly after arriving in California, her sister encouraged her to participate in a talent show at a local blues club. She won the contest and was approached by bluesman Johnny Otis, who added her to his roster of performers. He presented her as "Little Esther," and it has been said that she added "Phillips" after seeing a service station sign. She recorded on the Otis label for a few years, along with other labels. She recorded and performed, jazz, blues, R&B, gospel, and country and western. Phillips's music career, while successful, had its ups and downs due to her addictions. Among her greatest hits were "Mistrustin' Blues" and a remake of Dinah Washington's "What A Difference A Day Makes." (Courtesy of Tommie D. Boudreaux.)

Frederick Charles Tillis, PhD, was born in Galveston on January 5, 1930. He was exposed to music at a young age, courtesy of his musical mother. In elementary school, he joined the drum and bugle corps. Tillis performed with a jazz band when he was 12 years old. As a band student at Central High School, his teacher, Fleming S. Huff, suggested he play the saxophone. In 1946, Tillis enrolled in Wiley College on a music scholarship and, after graduation, was hired as the college's band director. In 1951, he enrolled in the University of Iowa for graduate study. He joined the US Air Force during the Korean War and became the director of the 356th Air Force Band. Later, he returned to his graduate studies, enrolling at the University of North Texas in Denton, where he studied music. After graduation, Tillis returned to the University of Iowa to finish his PhD. Upon completion in 1963, he taught at several colleges and universities. Tillis is a composer and has authored poetry and textbooks. (Courtesy of Old Central Cultural Center Inc.)

The Original Silverstone Quartet Singers was a group of local gospel singers who sang harmoniously throughout Texas and Louisiana from the late 1940s to the 1960s. Eural Stinson (second row, center), a well-known singer in Galveston County, was one of the lead singers. (Courtesy of the Eural Stinson family.)

Ruth Hall was born and raised in Galveston, graduating from Central High School in 1934. Hall played piano and violin at an early age and attended Prairie View University and Texas Southern University, majoring in elementary education and music with emphasis on organ and piano. She served as the musician for Avenue L Baptist Missionary Church for many years, and was the pianist for the Onzella singers, a female gospel group that traveled throughout Texas. Hall taught piano and was called upon for weddings, funerals, and special events at numerous churches. She was also the owner and director of a Kindergarten preschool for 40 years. (Courtesy of Rosenberg Library, Galveston.)

Oma Donal Galloway Jr. was born in Galveston on June 16, 1931, and was a 1947 graduate of Central High School. He served his country in the US Air Force during the Korean War and was the pianist with the 753rd Air Force Band. He earned his bachelor of music education degree at Texas Southern University and his master's degree in fine arts at Ohio State University. He was a member of Ohio University's Jazz Workshop, the School of Dance in Columbus, Ohio, the Amato Opera and Operetta Company in New York City, and the Music Academy of the West in Santa Barbara, California. His association with these organizations provided him with the opportunity to travel all over the world. (Courtesy of the Tremont House Hotel, Galveston.)

Eddie Curtis was born in Galveston on July 17, 1927. He was a singer, songwriter, composer, arranger, and playwright as well as a versatile instrumentalist. He started his own band at age 15. His higher education included Boston Conservatory of Music, Berklee School of Music, University of California at Los Angeles, and private lessons at Pepperdine University. Among the hundreds of songs he wrote or composed for many artists, the hit "Lovey Dovey" was recorded by the R&B group The Clovers, and "It Should've Been Me" was recorded by Ray Charles. Curtis also wrote several songs for Connie Francis, including her 1959 hit "You're Gonna Miss Me." (Courtesy of Bernard Curtis.)

Richard Gene Williams was born in Galveston on May 4, 1931, and was a 1947 graduate of Central High School. He was introduced to the tenor saxophone, but was encouraged by his high school band teacher to play the trumpet. He played with several local bands as a teenager before enrolling in Wiley College, majoring in music. Williams served in the Air Force from 1952 to 1956. After his discharge, he toured Europe with Lionel Hampton's band. After the tour, he enrolled in the Manhattan School of Music, earning his master's degree in music. He was a sideman with many bands, including Duke Ellington's Orchestra. He performed with pit orchestras on Broadway, playing the piccolo, trumpet, and flugelhorn. Williams also played on the original cast recording of *The Wiz*. His 1960 recording, "New Horn in Town," is the only recording under his name. (Courtesy of Lynette Williams.)

Clarence "Candy" Green was born on March 15, 1929, in Galveston. His mother introduced him to the piano at a young age. While his mother taught him to play spirituals, he preferred secular music. At the age of 15, he began playing in juke joints and brothels for tips. He soon became a well-known talent and was being paid for his performances. He traveled with the Merchant Navy from 1945 to 1948, but whenever he returned home, he would entertain at the same local establishments. In 1947, Green formed a band, and his "Galveston Blues" met with success in and around Galveston. Green and his combo also recorded "Green's Bounce," but the Houston recording studio went out of business before the records could be released. Shortly after this disappointing experience, the band broke up, but Green continued to perform in Texas and Louisiana. He recorded one of his most popular songs, "Hard Headed Woman" on the Peacock label in 1950, and recorded other songs under different labels. (Courtesy of Leon Banks Jr.)

Charles Brown (Tony Russell Brown), a native of Texas City, Texas, was born on September 13, 1922. Raised in Texas City by his maternal grandmother, he was a graduate of Central High School. His grandmother encouraged him to learn classical music and provided piano lessons. He was a member of Central's band and played the piano with his science teacher, who played saxophone with a local band. Brown earned a degree in chemistry from Prairie View College. After college, he was employed as a chemistry teacher in Baytown, Texas. Later, he was employed by the federal government in Arkansas and then as an apprentice electrician in Richmond, California. He finally settled in Los Angeles in 1943. In 1944, he won a talent show and was hired to play at Ivie's Chicken Shack. While working part-time at the Lincoln Theater, Jonny Moore offered Brown a job with his band, The Three Blazers. They recorded the hit "Driftin' Blues," featuring Brown on vocals. He recorded several more songs with Moore, including "Merry Christmas, Baby" in 1947. Brown left Moore and recorded several songs under his own name. (Courtesy of Old Central Cultural Center Inc.)

Camille HOWARD

VOL

X-TEMPORANEOUS BOOGIE

Camille Howard (Camille Agnes Browning) was born in Galveston on March 29, 1914, and attended Galveston's public schools. As a teenager, she played the piano and provided vocals with a local band, The Cotton Traven Trio, for five years. Howard then headed to the West Coast for greater opportunities. Shortly after arriving in California, she joined a small band, the Roy Milton Trio. By 1945, the group had expanded to seven members and recorded the hit "The R. M. Blues." The group changed its name to Roy Milton & His Solid Senders. After this success, still performing with Milton's band, Howard stepped out with the instrumental tune "Camille's Boogie" and the vocal "When I Grow Too Old To Dream." Other hits for the band featuring Howard on piano and as vocalist were "Thrill Me" and "Big Fat Mama." The president of the band's recording company, Specialty Records, decided it was time for Howard to record under her own name. Her first releases in 1948, the instrumental "X-Temporaneous Boogie" and the flip-side ballad "You Don't Love Me," were immediate hits, selling more than 100,000 copies. Howard continued to record and tour under her own name and with the Roy Milton band until the late 1950s. However, with the music world focused on rock 'n' roll, and her strong religious commitment, she ended her musical career. (Courtesy of Tommie D. Boudreaux.)

George Prader, a graduate of Central High School, was paralyzed in an automobile accident in 1930. Encouraged to do something with his life despite his disability, he decided to be a broadcaster and launched *The Harlem Express* on Galveston's KGBC radio. He broadcast his show daily from a hospital bed in front of a large window for more than 12 years. Big-name performers would visit George and give live interviews when they were in the Galveston area. It is believed that Prader introduced rock 'n' roll music to Galveston County. (Courtesy of Old Central Cultural Center Inc.)

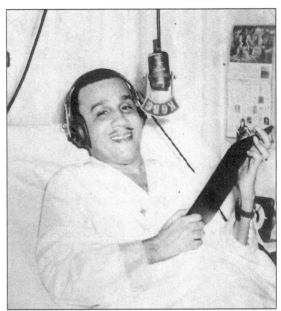

Jimmy Blair (James Williams Blair) was a sports and religion writer for the *Galveston Daily News*, beginning in 1949. A Galveston native, he attended elementary school in Madison, Wisconsin, graduated from Booker T. Washington High School in Houston, Texas, and attended Wilberforce University in Ohio for two years. Blair (second from right) wrote articles for the *Galveston Daily News* until the late 1980s. (Courtesy of Lee Arthur Gantt.)

G.T. Hogan (Wilbert Grandville Theodore Hogan, far left) was born on January 16, 1929, and graduated from Central High School in 1947. A sought-after drummer by popular bands around the country in the 1950s and 1960s, his credits on albums and records have been difficult to document, as he often altered his name. Music historians discovered that he signed on with bands as Granville Hogan, G.T. Hogan, Wilbert Hogan, Wilbert G.T. Hogan, and W.T. Hogan, among other names. He is credited with being featured on more than 50 albums through the early 1990s. (Courtesy of Leon Banks Jr.)

Members of The Ink Spots were all graduates of Central High School. Organized while still in school, the group continued to perform for several years in Galveston County and Houston. (Courtesy of Old Central Cultural Center Inc.)

During Reconstruction, Texas was occupied by Union forces from 1867 to 1873. On June 8, 1867, Maj. Gen. Charles Griffin, stationed in Galveston, not pleased with the local police, instructed Mayor James E. Haviland to dismiss the entire force. General Griffin then submitted to the mayor his own list of officers, which included the names of "five colored men." The mayor challenged the general's selection of the five African American officers. After several communications and meetings, Griffin dismissed Haviland and appointed Isaac G. Williams as the new mayor. The June 9, 1867, issue of *The Galveston Daily News* listed the first Galveston African American police officers as William Easton, Anderson Hunt, Simon Malone, Solomon Riley, and Robert Smith. (Courtesy of the Galveston Police Department.)

Officer William Menard Thomas Sr., born and raised in Galveston, became a police officer in 1918 and, by 1922, held the rank of sergeant. Thomas experienced the 1900 storm that destroyed Galveston and caused extensive damage to his church, Avenue L Baptist Church. He was among the members who replaced the church's stained-glass windows. The window with his name remains today. William Menard Thomas is a descendant of slaves owned by Galveston's founder, Michel Brananour Menard. (Courtesy of Scottie Stapleton and Wilella Kimble.)

MRS. ANNIE MAE CHARLES
Juvenile Officer
Galveston Police Dept.

Annie Mae Charles moved to Galveston in 1936. She was the first African American juvenile officer for the Galveston police department, a position she held from 1960 until 1977. (Courtesy of the City of Galveston Police Department.)

GENOICE WALKER
HOSE & LADDERMAN

LUCIOUS POPE
HOSE & LADDERMAN

LEROY L. SMALL
HOSE & LADDERMAN

The first African American firemen in Galveston were Genoice Walker, Lucious Pope, and Leroy Small. They were among the eight hose-and-ladder members added to the Galveston Fire Department on Thursday, November 21, 1957, by the board of the city commissioners, on recommendation of police and fire commissioner Walter B. Rourke. (Courtesy of the City of Galveston Fire Department.)

Jack Johnson (John Arthur Johnson), the first African American heavyweight champion of the world, was born in Galveston on March 31, 1878. He dropped out of school around the sixth or seventh grade to be a dockworker on Galveston's wharf. His fighting skills were noted when he was a teenager. His debut as a professional fighter occurred in Galveston on November 1, 1897. As he continued to fight and win, his colorful lifestyle did not sit well with many people, especially whites. He was finally arrested for violating the Mann Act, which prohibited "transporting women across state lines for immoral purposes." Johnson skipped bail and left the United States, but returned and served his sentence. While incarcerated, he made improvements on a wrench and was issued a patent for his invention on April 18, 1922 (US Patent No. 1,413,121). Johnson continued to fight into his sixties, mostly exhibitions to earn money. He died in a car accident on June 10, 1946. (Courtesy of the Library of Congress.)

Ray Dohn Dillon was born in Tylertown, Mississippi, on September 22, 1929, and moved to Galveston with his family at a young age. He graduated from Central High School in 1948. He was an outstanding athlete in high school and at Prairie View College, where he earned his degree in physical education. In 1952, Dillon was the first African American from Galveston to be drafted into the National Football League. He played with the Detroit Lions at various positions before moving on to Ontario and the Hamilton Tiger-Cats of the Canadian Football League. In 1953, under coach Carl Voyles, the Tigers-Cats won the Grey Cup championship. A knee injury ended Dillon's professional football career. When he returned home, he was hired by the city of Galveston as the recreation director for Norris Wright Cuney Recreational Center, remaining there until 1957. Dillon was then hired by Galveston Independent School District, where he taught swimming and coached football under head coach Ray T. Sheppard at Central High School. With the merging of the two schools in 1968, Ball High became the only public high school in Galveston. That year, Dillon was appointed to the department of human relations and attendance and as chief of the district's police department. (Courtesy of the Ray Dohn Dillon family.)

Charley Ferguson (Charles Edward Ferguson) was born in 1939 in Dallas, Texas. He and his family moved to Galveston, where he graduated from Central High School in 1957. Ferguson was an outstanding athlete at Central and at Tennessee State University. He was drafted into the National Football League in 1961 by the Cleveland Browns, and in 1962 played for the Minnesota Vikings. He was traded to the Buffalo Bills of the American Football League in 1963 and played with the team until his retirement in 1969. He remained in Buffalo after his playing days. Ferguson was in playoff games for four straight years with the Bills, including 1964 and 1965 when the team won the AFL championship. In 1965, he was named an AFL All-Star. (Courtesy of Frederick Ferguson.)

Joel B. "Baby Joe" Smith Jr. was born in Galveston on August 17, 1939, and was a 1957 graduate of Central High School. He attended Prairie View A&M University and earned a degree in industrial education. Smith played in the American Football League for one year and in the Canadian Football League in 1962 and 1963. After his football career, he returned to Galveston and taught industrial arts at Central High School for several years, later starting his own construction business. Smith's high school classmate, Benjamin Mays—a graduate of Texas Southern University—also played for the Canadian Football League. (Courtesy of the Joel B. Smith Jr. family.)

The "Bruiser"

EDWARD MITCHELL

Edward Levine Mitchell was born on September 5, 1942, and graduated from Central High School in 1960. He attended Nebraska University and Southern University before being drafted by the AFL's San Diego Chargers in 1965. Mitchell played with the Chargers through 1966 and with the Houston Oilers in 1967. (Courtesy of Old Central Cultural Center Inc.)

Stanley Waverly Thomas Jr. was born on February 4, 1947, and graduated from Central High School in 1965. Outstanding in track and field, he won a scholarship to Lamar Tech College (Lamar University) in Beaumont, Texas. He was the first African American to join the school's track team, winning many awards. However, on April 1, 1968, tragedy struck the team while flying back from a track meet. The airplane crashed in Beaumont and all members of the team died, including the coach. (Courtesy of Irene Thomas Young and Floretta Thomas Laws.)

Leon Phillips Sr. worked as a longshoreman
for ILA Local 1504. In 1943, he was the
first African American in Galveston to
become a foreman for the local's railroad
gang. (Courtesy of Leon Phillips Jr.)

In 1945, Georgia Harris Batiste
became the first African American
female to be hired by the
custodial department of Galveston
Independent School District.
(Courtesy of Sherman Batiste Boyer.)

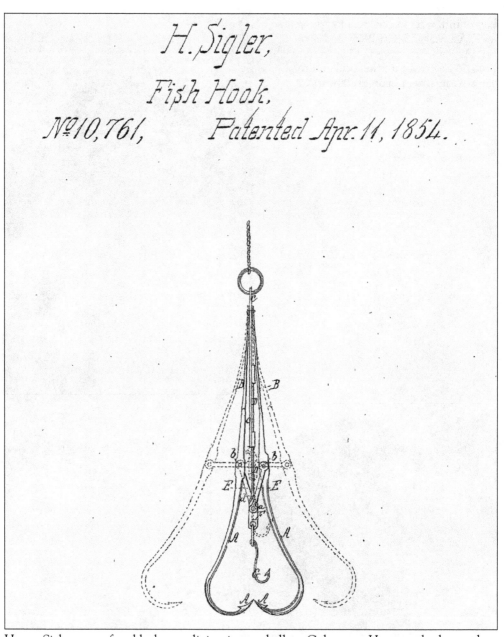

H. Sigler,
Fish Hook.
Nº 10,761,   Patented Apr. 11, 1854.

Henry Sigler was a free black man living in antebellum Galveston. He was a barber and an inventor who patented a more efficient fishhook in 1854. In 1858, he sold the design to a group of businessmen in New Orleans for $625. (Courtesy of University of North Texas Libraries, UNT Libraries Government Documents Department.)

Cornelia Harris (center) graduated from Central High School in 1965 and attended Pepperdine University in Malibu, California, where she received her undergraduate and master's degrees. She was the first African American woman elected to the Galveston City Council and the first African American woman to be named mayor pro-tem for the city. In 1957, Holy Rosary Parish named Harris the Queen of Mardi Gras (pictured). (Courtesy of Cornelia Harris Banks.)

World War I veteran Enoch Withers went to work for W.L. Moody Jr. in 1919 after being discharged from the US Army. Withers served the family for over 50 years before his retirement in the 1970s. He took pride in his dapper appearance, insisting, "A man is judged first for his appearance and then for how he speaks." While he had no children of his own, nieces and nephews remember sitting on the floor around him as he told stories about Galveston and his travels with the Moody family. When advanced age and declining health took a toll on him, Withers moved to Port Arthur to be near family. He passed away in 1988 at the age of 98 and was buried in his beloved Galveston. (Courtesy of the Center for 20th Century Texas Studies.)

World War II veteran Rev. James B. Thomas (1924–2007) was a civil rights leader and 1943 graduate of Central High School who worked tirelessly to improve the lives of Galveston's African American citizens. In 1959, Thomas was one of the plaintiffs in a lawsuit filed by W.J. Durham, Thomas Dent, and Thurgood Marshall—then a New York attorney representing the National Association for the Advancement of Colored People (NAACP)—petitioning for integration of the Galveston Independent School District. Their day in court came in January 1961 with Judge Ben Connally ruling in their favor. A few days later, GISD opened the school year implementing gradual integration throughout the district. From 1979 to 1982, Thomas served as president of the Galveston Chapter of the NAACP, which had been organized in November 1918. During his tenure as president, Thomas and former state representative Al Edwards played an important role in establishing Juneteenth as an official state holiday. (Courtesy of Reverend James B. Thomas family.)

Doug Matthews was born in Galveston on January 31, 1951, and attended Galveston's public schools, graduating from the newly integrated Ball High School in 1969. In the late 1960s, the school district, still under court order to integrate, implemented "Freedom of Choice" for all grade levels. After attending Central High School for three years, Matthews chose to attend the predominately white Ball High School during his senior year, where he became the first African American to serve as vice president of the student council. An honor student, Matthews excelled in sports and was one of two African American captains of the Ball High School football team, which was undefeated that year, earning a slot in the state semi-final game. Matthews was selected the "Most Scholarly Player" and offered a scholarship to attend Lamar University in Beaumont, Texas, where he majored in government. After graduating from Lamar, Matthews went to work for the city of Galveston and later became the first African American city manager in the state. He currently serves as the assistant vice president for governmental affairs at the University of Texas Medical Branch, Galveston. (Courtesy of Doug Matthews.)

About Galveston Historical Foundation

Incorporated in 1954, Galveston Historical Foundation (GHF) is one of the nation's largest local preservation organizations. During the past 50 years, the foundation has expanded its mission to encompass community redevelopment, public education, historic preservation advocacy, maritime preservation, and stewardship of historic properties. Today, the foundation has more than 2,000 memberships, representing individuals, families, and businesses across Texas, the United States, and abroad. GHF exerts a profound impact on the culture and economy of Galveston.

The foundation has earned praise from prominent state and national organizations. Among its recognized efforts are the redevelopment of The Strand, the rescue and restoration of the 1877 iron barque *Elissa*, the revitalization of historic residential neighborhoods and creation of historic districts, and the conception of signature events, including Dickens on The Strand and the Galveston Historic Homes Tour.

Galveston Historical Foundation serves as the steward and operator of many of Galveston's most significant historic properties, including the 1838 Michel Menard House, 1839 Samuel May Williams House, 1859 Ashton Villa, 1859 St. Joseph's German Catholic Church, 1861 Custom House, 1880 Garten Verein, 1877 tall ship *Elissa*, 1892 Bishop's Palace, 1911 Rosewood Cemetery, and the 1937 shrimp boat *Santa Maria*.

The foundation continues to be a driving force in the development and enrichment of the city of Galveston. The foundation is a major voice of preservation advocacy both locally and throughout the state. GHF's many departments, programs, events, and volunteers are dedicated to its mission: preserving and revitalizing the architectural, cultural, and maritime heritage of Galveston Island for the enrichment of all.

Visit us at
arcadiapublishing.com

Printed in the USA
CPSIA information can be obtained
at www.ICGtesting.com
LVHW081144221223
766782LV00085B/163